Data Protection and the Cloud

Are you really managing the risks?

Second edition

Data Protection and the Cloud

Are you really managing the risks?

Second edition

PAUL TICHER

IT Governance Publishing

IT Governance Publishing Ltd
Unit 3, Clive Court
Bartholomew's Walk
Cambridgeshire Business Park
Ely, Cambridgeshire
CB7 4EA
United Kingdom
www.itgovernancepublishing.co.uk

First published in the United Kingdom in 2015 by IT Governance Publishing – ISBN 978-1-84928-712-8

Second edition published in the United Kingdom in 2018 by IT Governance Publishing – ISBN 978-1-78778-028-6

ABOUT THE AUTHOR

With a background in IT, focused on CRM and other information management applications, Paul has worked in data protection for more than 20 years. He is now a well-known consultant on the topic, mainly to non-profit organisations, and specialises in work with charities and voluntary organisations.

Paul is the author of the standard work *Data Protection for Voluntary Organisations* as well as materials for ITGP and other publishers. He also carries out data protection reviews and delivers training and webinars on the topic.

ACKNOWLEDGEMENTS

I would like to thank Chris Evans, IT service management specialist; Christopher Wright, Wright-CandA Consulting Ltd, author of *Agile Governance and Audit*; and ir. H.L. (Maarten) Souw RE, enterprise risk and QA manager, UWV, for their helpful comments during the review process.

CONTENTS

INTRODUCTION

This book is intended to be an introduction to the risks involved in Cloud sourcing, to enable managers to ask the right questions. Suggestions are offered for the kind of risks an organisation's use of the Cloud might generate, and the remedial measures that might be taken. These are given as examples only and are not intended to be a substitute for qualified legal or technical advice. Other publications from ITGP, listed at the end of this book, address security in more detail.

Cloud security has to be a joint effort between the provider and the customer. The customer must select a provider with adequate security and other provisions; many of the topics discussed here will therefore be of equal interest to Cloud providers. However, the customer's responsibilities go further. Without a well-functioning information security process in place, selection of a secure Cloud provider is only a half measure.

In order to emphasise where the responsibility for data protection compliance normally lies, the Cloud services customer is more or less interchangeably referred to in this publication as the 'data controller'.

This pocket guide is based on EU legislation, and will therefore be of relevance to any organisation that needs to meet the EU General Data Protection Regulation's (GDPR) requirements.

CHAPTER 1: BACKGROUND

One of the most dramatic recent developments in computing has been the rapid adoption of Cloud applications. There is no sign of this diminishing with the increasing proliferation of small, mobile devices that presuppose always-on Internet connections and rely heavily on the Cloud.

The business advantages of the Cloud are clear, both for the provider and the user. The provider can move to a subscription model for occasional as well as frequent users. The user gets the flexibility of being able to access both data and applications from any location, avoids much of the burden of applying security or productivity upgrades to their software and has the option of multi-platform access to an integrated set of data.

Cloud usage is continuing to expand. The 2018 Bitglass Cloud Adoption report shows that the percentage of organisations having adopted the Cloud in some form is more than 81%; in 2014, this was only 24%.[1] What's more, highly confidential and business-critical data is routinely placed in the Cloud. Considering that the report also shows that, on average, only a quarter of Cloud-using organisations use single sign-on (SSO) as a basic Cloud security measure, this is worrying.

As with all technologies, the legal and practical implications are not always immediately apparent, and unexpected problems can crop up. Cloud computing is evolving much quicker than laws can, meaning that it does not always sit easily within such legislation. The EU Directive 95/46/EC – also known as the Data Protection Directive (DPD) – was agreed in 1995, making it the main reference point on data protection for 21 years. At the time it was agreed, the World Wide Web was in its infancy, but when

---

[1] Bitglass, "Cloud Adoption 2018 War", _https://pages.bitglass.com/FY18BR-CloudAdoption_LP.html_.

the DPD was superseded by the GDPR in May 2018 (which was agreed in 2016) it was well out of date.

At about the same time, EU Directive 2016/1148, also known as the Directive on security of network and information systems (NIS Directive), was transposed into and enforced through member states' national laws. Organisations within scope are required to put technical and organisational measures in place that will protect them from cyber attacks and ensure they are able to respond in the event of disruption.

Data protection obligations

Failing to adequately protect data can have serious consequences. First and foremost, of course, the individuals whose data was breached will be affected. Although the cases where serious physical harm has been directly caused through a failure to prevent data falling into the wrong hands are thankfully rare, they have nevertheless still occurred. Other types of damage, including financial, are more common – some of the more obvious ones being fines and lost turnover through reputational damage. The latter can seriously impact brand integrity and customer loyalty, fuelled by the publicity given to serious breaches, if relatively recent cases such as Equifax[2] and Facebook[3] are anything to go by.

The ease with which data can be moved around the web and the user's day-to-day (in fact, second-to-second) reliance on the performance of Cloud providers make data protection compliance more challenging than it might be when data is

---

[2] Rebecca Hill, "Exposing 145m Equifax customer deets: \$240m. Legal fees: \$28.9m. Insurance: Priceless", *The Register*, April 2018, *www.theregister.co.uk/2018/04/27/equifax_breach_cost_240m_to_date*
.

[3] Olivia Solon and Oliver Laughland, "Cambridge Analytica closing after Facebook data harvesting scandal", *The Guardian*, May 2018, *www.theguardian.com/uk-news/2018/may/02/cambridge-analytica-closing-down-after-facebook-row-reports-say*.

sitting firmly under control on an in-house server. The GDPR and NIS Directive address some of these challenges but it is unlikely that they or any other legislation can remove the risks inherent in Cloud computing.

Having said that, if these risks are managed properly, they need not be showstoppers. The benefits of Cloud computing are certainly tempting. The important thing is to be fully aware of the risks and take appropriate action before deciding to put valuable, confidential data into the Cloud.

Changes introduced by the GDPR

Data protection – a much-discussed topic – has been heightened since the enforcement of the GDPR. The changes introduced by the Regulation include, for starters, the fact that it is a regulation, rather than a directive; it therefore directly applies to all organisations that handle EU residents' personal data.

The fact that it is now a regulation is not the only big change. For one, the range of personal data covered is now much broader. Data subjects are also given much more control over their data with expanded rights; for instance, they may request a copy of any personal data held on them without charge (the right of access), and may ask for data to be transmitted to another data controller (the right to data portability). If your organisation stores any such data in the Cloud, this change may have significant implications.

However, many fundamentals of data protection have remained the same, even if the contents have been reshuffled and/or set out in more detail. Ultimately, the Regulation boils down to a small number of core principles and data subjects' rights, which organisations must consider when implementing or using any technology, especially if those technologies operate remotely, such as in the Cloud.

The NIS Directive

Unlike regulations, directives are legal instruments that set minimum standards and parameters for EU member states to implement on a local level. Although there may be differences in each state's implementation, a minimum standard will nonetheless be maintained. One relatively recent – and very relevant – example for Cloud providers and users is the NIS Directive.

The NIS Directive applies to two main groups: operators of essential services (OES) – in other words, critical infrastructure – and digital service providers (DSPs) – encompassing online marketplaces, online search engines and Cloud service providers.

The Directive was introduced by the EU in response to the growing number of cyber attacks on critical infrastructure. Such digital attacks can significantly impact the physical world and prevent access to services that are essential for both business and society. To give an example, in 2015 Ukraine was the victim of what is believed to be the first successful attack against a power grid, leaving 230,000 people without power for up to six hours.[4]

DSPs, such as Cloud providers, are also covered by the NIS Directive because their services are essential for critical infrastructure organisations – as well as other businesses and individuals – to function. Additionally, because of their cross-border nature, the Directive is meant to apply to DSPs without exception or national variance, which is achieved through the European Commission's (EC) Implementing Regulation.

This is good news for Cloud users: knowing that providers are legally required to put measures in place that ensure both the security and availability of their services is reassuring. However, organisations using the Cloud do need to consider the GDPR and how to comply with it. They also need to ensure that any technology placed in the Cloud is secure in the first place – otherwise, securing the Cloud would only be a half measure.

---

[4] Kim Zetter, "Inside the Cunning, Unprecedented Hack of Ukraine's Power Grid", *Wired*, March 2016, *www.wired.com/2016/03/inside-cunning-unprecedented-hack-ukraines-power-grid/*.

CHAPTER 2: DEFINITIONS

Cloud technologies are governed by a number of laws, so it is useful to understand a few key terms from the GDPR and the NIS Directive.[5]

Cloud computing service (NIS Directive)

> a digital service that enables access to a scalable and elastic pool of shareable computing resources

Note that this is the *legal* definition; there may be services that do not necessarily meet this definition but are still advertised as operating in the 'Cloud', and for your purposes it may be worth treating them as such.

Data controller (GDPR)

> the natural or legal person, public authority, agency or other body which, alone or jointly with others, determines the purposes and means of the processing of personal data; where the purposes and means of such processing are determined by Union or Member State law, the controller or the specific criteria for its nomination may be provided for by Union or Member State law

In other words, the entities that determine what the data is processed for and how it is processed. These will usually be the 'public-facing' entities that data subjects supply their information to.

---

[5] All definitions can be found in Article 4 of the GDPR and the NIS Directive.

Data processor (GDPR)

> a natural or legal person, public authority, agency or other body which processes personal data on behalf of the controller

The data processor is the entity actually processing the data. In many cases, the data controller and the data processor will be the same entity, although a single data controller may have several data processors. If you use a Cloud service provider, your relationship may well be a processor–controller one, with the Cloud provider as the processor. In particular, if you store data in the Cloud, that will be considered processing under the GDPR, making that Cloud provider a processor. There are many grey areas, however, and the specifics – whether the provider is a processor or simply a 'third party' – are often down to the exact service provided.

Data subject (GDPR)

> an identifiable natural person is one who can be identified, directly or indirectly, in particular by reference to an identifier such as a name, an identification number, location data, an online identifier or to one or more factors specific to the physical, physiological, genetic, mental, economic, cultural or social identity of that natural person

The list of identifiers above is not exhaustive: *any* information, in *any* format, capable of identifying a data subject is deemed personal data. This includes any correspondence, photographs and CCTV footage – whether stored in the Cloud or not. Note that the consequence of this definition is that you do not even need to know someone's name; if you can single them out and perhaps treat them differently from anyone else, this would likely make them 'identifiable'. An online persona may bear no relation to a person's name in the real world, but the information held about them is still likely to be personal data.

Note also that nationality is of no importance; the data subject is protected by the GDPR as long as they are an EU resident.

Digital service provider (NIS Directive)

> any legal person that provides a digital service

A "digital service" is, in turn, defined as "any service normally provided for remuneration, at a distance, by electronic means and at the individual request of a recipient of services". The organisations considered DSPs are Cloud service providers, online marketplaces and online search engines.

Incident (NIS Directive)

> any event having an actual adverse effect on the security of network and information systems

All incidents are 'events', but not all events have negative consequences. It is common to investigate all events to determine whether they are actually incidents.

Personal data (GDPR)

> any information relating to an identified or identifiable natural person ('data subject')

A data subject can only be a *living person* – the Regulation does not cover the deceased, corporations or other entities.

Personal data breach (GDPR)

> a breach of security leading to the accidental or unlawful destruction, loss, alteration, unauthorised disclosure of, or access to, personal data transmitted, stored or otherwise processed

The majority of data breaches that the GDPR is concerned with are personal data breaches. This differs from the NIS Directive, which is primarily interested in disruptions that affect the availability of essential services.

Processing (GDPR)

> any operation or set of operations which is performed on personal data or on sets of personal data, whether or not by

> automated means, such as collection, recording, organisation, structuring, storage, adaptation or alteration, retrieval, consultation, use, disclosure by transmission, dissemination or otherwise making available, alignment or combination, restriction, erasure or destruction

This is an extremely broad definition but, again, it is not exhaustive. Functionally, processing may include any interaction you have with personal data, in whatever form it takes. As such, it is hard to see how a Cloud application could operate without 'processing' data within this definition.

Special categories of personal data (GDPR)

> personal data revealing racial or ethnic origin, political opinions, religious or philosophical beliefs, or trade-union membership, and the processing of genetic data, biometric data for the purpose of uniquely identifying a natural person, data concerning health or data concerning a natural person's sex life or sexual orientation[6]

Such data, also referred to as 'sensitive data', is not allowed to be processed except under specific circumstances. If such an exception applies, the data will require special treatment. In terms of Cloud computing, the loss or compromise of sensitive personal data would be a very serious matter. Organisations need to therefore be especially certain about how such data is processed; it could, for instance, have an impact on the use of Cloud services or the decision on whether a Cloud approach is appropriate.

Third party (GDPR)

> a natural or legal person, public authority, agency or body other than the data subject, controller, processor and persons

---

[6] GDPR, Article 9(1).

who, under the direct authority of the controller or processor, are authorised to process personal data

As mentioned earlier, it may be tricky to establish whether the Cloud service you use can be considered a processor or third party. However, your Cloud provider should be able to help establish the precise details of the relationship.

CHAPTER 3: THE DATA CONTROLLER/DATA PROCESSOR RELATIONSHIP

Responsibility for compliance with the data processing principles and other aspects of the GDPR lies with the data controller (as defined in the previous chapter).

It is important to note that group-level responsibility for data protection compliance is not an option. Each legal entity – company, public body, institution, partnership or even an unincorporated charity – carries its own, separate responsibility.

The Cloud provider in many cases will be a data processor (also as previously defined), particularly if you store data in the Cloud. However, as discussed in the previous chapter, there may be cases where the Cloud provider is merely a 'third party'. Either way, if you are the data controller, you must ensure that the Cloud provider processes personal data on your instructions only.

Although it would ultimately be for the courts to determine the exact role of a Cloud provider, it is always useful to establish a common view between the customer and the Cloud provider on what the relationship appears to be, as a basis for clarifying their respective responsibilities.

Where a data controller employs the services of a data processor or third party, responsibility for data protection compliance remains with the data controller.[7] If data is lost in the Cloud, or if security is breached, the data controller is responsible for any harm caused to the individuals whose data it decided to place in the Cloud, and could be the subject of enforcement action taken by the supervisory authority.

---

[7] Unless the data processor or third party acts outside of the instructions of the data controller or otherwise breaches the GDPR.

Data controller–processor contracts

The GDPR is specific in its approach to the relationship between the organisation that carries the responsibility – the data controller – and any organisation to which work is outsourced – the data processor.

The Regulation requires there to be a "contract or other legal act between the controller and the processor", setting out the relationship and imposing security obligations on the data processor. The GDPR states in Article 28(4) that such a legal act should provide "sufficient guarantees to implement appropriate technical and organisational measures" to meet its requirements. The data controller is also explicitly given the responsibility for assessing the adequacy of the data processor's security and taking steps to verify it.

If there is any possibility, therefore, that the Cloud provider is a data processor, it would be very unwise for the customer (in this case, the controller) to proceed without a written contract that meets at least the minimum provisions in the GDPR.

Where Cloud services are provided on a bespoke basis, they may be the subject of contractual negotiations between the data controller and data processor. In such instances a contract can be drawn up that unequivocally meets the requirements of the Regulation.

However, in many cases – even for large business deals – the contract for Cloud services is set out in non-negotiable terms and conditions, or with very little scope for variation. If the Cloud provider does not offer terms and conditions that meet the GDPR's requirements, there is little that can be done to get them added in.

Ideally, a data processor contract should also provide indemnity for the data controller against any costs resulting from the data processor's failure to deliver. At the very least, the controller needs to provide clear instructions for the processor, including contract clauses making it clear that the processor is liable for any breaches as a result of not following the controller's explicit instructions when processing personal data. This is not a legal requirement but makes sound commercial sense. The standard terms and conditions for Cloud services almost inevitably exclude any indemnity for a failure of the service, of course.

This does not mean, however, that the data controller should accept the data processor's terms uncritically. They should be examined carefully to ensure that no unacceptable risks are being taken. If there are gaps, it may be necessary to consider additional measures that should be taken on the customer side to compensate for any deficiencies in the terms and conditions on offer from the supplier.

One particular concern should be the possibility that the Cloud provider subcontracts parts of its service, which may not be apparent from service descriptions or architectural diagrams. This subcontracting must be approved by the controller under Article 28(2) of the GDPR. As controller, you will need at least some understanding of how the Cloud architecture works in order to determine whether any other parties constitute sub-processors. The customer must be able to rely on the whole chain providing the necessary quality of service. Some of these links may be outside the EU or, more pertinently, outside the European Economic Area (EEA), which brings additional data protection considerations.

Following is a quick checklist for issues that a data processor contract (or terms and conditions) with a Cloud provider should ideally address if the application makes, or could make, any use of personal data. Please note that the list is not intended to be a complete or accurate description of the provisions that should be in a contract between the data controller and a Cloud-based data processor, and some of the points may not be relevant in every case.

1) Is it clear that the customer is the data controller and the Cloud provider is a data processor?
2) Is it clear what processing the Cloud provider is expected or entitled to carry out on the data controller's data?
3) Is it explicit that all the customer's data supplied is confidential (unless it is legitimately in the public domain), and that the Cloud provider is not to process the data or disclose except on the data controller's instruction,

or retain it after the contract ends or the data controller stops using the service?

4) Does the Cloud provider have adequate technical and organisational measures in place for effective security, and can the data controller audit this effectively?

5) Is there a requirement for the Cloud provider to inform the data controller immediately of any security breach they become aware of (whether they caused it or not)?

6) Does the Cloud provider indemnify the data controller for any costs incurred in rectifying data breaches brought about deliberately or negligently by the Cloud provider (ideally including costs of reassuring affected individuals, even if this is not legally required)?

7) Is the Cloud provider required not to do anything that would put the data controller in breach of the GDPR?

8) Is the Cloud provider required to promptly forward all requests from data subjects exercising their rights, including data subject access requests (DSARs), and complaints about any of the processing to the data controller?

9) Is the Cloud provider required not to process the data, or allow it to be processed, outside the EEA (unless the data controller gives prior consent to do so)?

10) Is the Cloud provider prohibited from subcontracting any processing (or not to do so without the data controller's prior consent)?

CHAPTER 4: SECURITY OF PROCESSING

Security is one of the most important safeguards in preventing harm to individuals, as reflected in Article 32 of the GDPR, which mandates "appropriate technical and organisational measures to ensure a level of security appropriate to the risk".

Specifically, it requires organisations to identify and mitigate "risks that are presented by [data] processing, in particular from accidental or unlawful destruction, loss, alteration, unauthorised disclosure of, or access to personal data transmitted, stored or otherwise processed". Such 'appropriate' measures may include:

- Encrypting personal data;
- Ensuring your processing systems and service are secure and resilient;
- Being able to restore availability and access to personal data within a reasonable timeframe after an incident has occurred; and
- Implementing a process that continually assesses the performance and effectiveness of your implemented technical and organisational measures.

'Organisational' security measures should always include attention to people and processes. Human error and process failures are regularly significant underlying causes for data breaches.[8] The data protection liability, however, rests with the organisation.

---

[8] The supervisory authority in the UK, the Information Commissioner's Office (ICO), publishes quarterly figures of reported breaches at _https://ico.org.uk/action-weve-taken/data-security-incident-trends_, which show this pattern.

Confidentiality, integrity and availability

The requirements in Article 32 of the GDPR to prevent unauthorised destruction, loss, alteration or access closely mirror the three standard aims of best-practice information security: confidentiality, integrity and availability.

Confidentiality is concerned with setting limits on who may have access to specified information, based on their need to know. In a personal data context, 'need to know' means that the data should only be processed for the purposes specified by the data controller to the data subject. As the Cloud provider is likely to not have any reason to even need access, data should be protected, e.g. by client-side encryption, before it even enters the Cloud provider's physical infrastructure. Any breach of confidentiality in respect of personal data is likely to be unauthorised access, which the measures outlined in Article 32 should aim to prevent.

In maintaining confidentiality, it is unwise to rely on the probity, conscientiousness or common sense of all those who may handle or have access to data, even if they know the confidentiality boundaries. Technical security measures to prevent unauthorised access should therefore be concerned with not merely preventing deliberate external intrusion; they should also aim to limit access by authorised users to just the information they actually 'need to know'. Segmentation of data supported by a robust system of access credentials is one of the key controls in this respect.

Data integrity implies that once data has been entered into the system, it should not be modified in an unintended or unauthorised way. This is a very straightforward element of preventing "alteration" – which, if unauthorised or unintended, constitutes a data breach under the GDPR.

Availability relates to loss and destruction. The concept, however, goes beyond the permanent non-availability that would result from loss of data, to include the requirement for the information to be available whenever it is needed.

Data in transit and at rest

Data 'in transit' is always more vulnerable than data 'at rest'. It is inherent in Cloud computing that data will spend more time in transit than it would if it were being processed on an in-house system. Processing personal data in the Cloud therefore automatically exposes it to greater risks than it would face behind securely run perimeter defences of an on-site installation.

That is not to say that the data faces no risks if held on site: it would still be vulnerable to misuse by authorised users, to loss or damage if the backup regime is inadequate, or to external intrusion. In some respects, the Cloud provider may actually offer greater protection against a backup failure or a poorly implemented firewall.

However, the IBM X-Force Threat Intelligence Index 2018 survey found that misconfigured Cloud servers were responsible for almost 70% of all compromised records tracked by X-Force in 2017.[9] This included some extremely sensitive data, which was stored in the Cloud without the users' knowledge.

There are also regular reports of large amounts of personal data being stolen from online locations. Websites are likely to be particularly vulnerable because, by their very nature, they are designed to have at least an element of public exposure. A website is often the gateway to a large online database of site users, and an integral part of an organisation's relationship with its customers or service users.

Cloud applications that are not intended to be publicly accessible avoid one obvious avenue for compromise, but that does not make them immune to security risks. Intrusion is still a possibility. Technical problems could also cause a loss of

---

[9] IBM, "IBM X-Force Threat Intelligence Index 2018 – Notable security events of 2017, and a look ahead", March 2018, *http://www-01.ibm.com/common/ssi/cgi-bin/ssialias?htmlfid=77014377USEN*.

integrity if the interruption occurs while data is in transit, and any loss or corruption of data is not detected and rectified.

Security in the Cloud

Security has to be present throughout, from the device through which the user accesses the application, to the depths of the Cloud provider's system – for which the entire responsibility lies with the data controller. Normally, as discussed above, the data controller is the customer, with the Cloud provider acting as a data processor or third party.

It is emphatically not enough for the data controller to make assumptions about the security measures that may – or may not – have been taken by the Cloud provider. One clear example of this is the case of the British Pregnancy Advisory Service (BPAS). In February 2014, BPAS was fined £200,000 (about €230,000) by the UK's ICO after its website was hacked.[10] It is interesting to note that the BPAS considered the fine "out of proportion" at the time, although it is now well below the significantly higher maximum fines of the GDPR.

In the breach, highly confidential messages from almost 10,000 people, sent via the website to BPAS, were stolen – a task made relatively easy by basic security weaknesses on its website. This exploit was intended to undermine BPAS but could also have placed many of the individuals at considerable personal risk if, as was threatened, the messages had been made public by the criminal hacker.

In imposing the penalty, the ICO made it clear that it was the responsibility of BPAS to instruct the web designers and web hosts to implement adequate security, and check that they did so – not just to rely on the assumption that it would be done. BPAS failed to replace the default administrator password, therefore clearly not meeting its responsibilities as data controller, even

---

[10] BBC News, "Abortion provider BPAS fined £200,000 for data breach", March 2014, *www.bbc.co.uk/news/health-26479985*.

though it felt the fine was "out of proportion", as BPAS considered itself "a victim of a serious crime". That may well have been the case, but – if anything – is even more reason to ensure the security of any processors and third parties it uses.

Additional risks from 'bring your own device' (BYOD) – or 'application' – policies

One of the clear benefits of Cloud computing is the possibility of easy (and cheap) access anywhere that you have an Internet connection. This is often an ideal solution for mobile workers, remote offices and home working. However, users may find reasons for wanting to gain access from personal devices rather than company ones, and the number of devices capable of gaining access has increased rapidly. Desktop computers, laptops, tablets and smartphones all bring their own risks.

It is not within the scope of this pocket guide to provide an exhaustive list of all the issues to address in a BYOD policy, but those particularly relevant to Cloud computing include:

- Controlling access to the device;
- Users other than the owner;
- Vulnerabilities introduced by other applications on the device;
- Opportunities to download data onto the device;
- Action to be taken in the event that the device is compromised; and
- Use of insecure Cloud applications to transfer data to or from the device.

Actions that can be taken to mitigate each of these risks are discussed in the next chapter.

Even where the data controller officially makes no use of Cloud applications, a BYOD policy must address the issue of whether the device owner is permitted to use personal Cloud-based accounts to transfer data to and from the device, or to work on material that is held on the device. Personal accounts, especially if they can be signed up to at no charge, may well not provide the same levels of security or service availability that business-oriented and paid-for accounts can offer. Surveys regularly suggest that this type of 'shadow' Cloud use is widespread. Where the data controller has corporate accounts with more secure applications, these should be used in preference.

The experience of Aberdeen City Council is instructive.[11] In 2011, a social worker was permitted to work from home. She had attended a case conference and was typing up the report on her home computer. She was apparently unaware that the folder in which she stored the document on her computer was set up to synchronise automatically with a Cloud-based location.

A colleague who had attended the same case conference happened to search for his name and job title on the web several months later, only to find that the document appeared. There was no security in place to prevent anyone accessing this highly confidential material.

The Council was fined £100,000, even though neither the computer nor the Cloud service was directly under its control. When the employee was authorised to work on confidential material at home, the Council should have ensured that appropriate security measures were in place.

---

[11] Warwick Ashford, "Aberdeen City Council gets £100,000 penalty for IT security failings", *Computer Weekly*, August 2013, www.computerweekly.com/news/2240204497/Aberdeen-City-Council-gets-100000-penalty-for-IT-security-failings.

CHAPTER 5: MITIGATING SECURITY RISKS IN THE CLOUD

Effectively mitigating security risks requires a range of measures to be implemented together and used in combination, in order to provide the end-to-end security discussed in the previous chapter. This pocket guide will not give a detailed description of the technical measures available, and readers with more technical expertise may well be aware of other measures that are perhaps more appropriate for their situation.

Security – like other aspects of data protection – is not something that should be added as an afterthought. Security should be built into an organisation's infrastructure and become part of how the organisation does business in every respect. Moving to the Cloud does not solve the problem if an organisation's existing security architecture and infrastructure is not up to standard – it just adds another element that must be addressed.

Most Cloud providers are acutely aware that security must be a high priority, both for them and their customers. They typically stress the degree to which they take security seriously, and many claim that their security is likely to be considerably better than in most small organisations and some larger ones. This is possibly true, but Cloud providers may also be a more tempting target, and breaches leading to unauthorised access, as we have seen, undoubtedly do occur. This should not be too surprising, as any organisation could be breached, given enough attempts and resources.

Cloud security must cover *all* risks addressed in Article 32 of the GDPR – not just preventing unauthorised access, but also preventing accidental or unlawful destruction, loss and alteration of personal data. Many Cloud providers offer indications of the level of service they aim to provide – and may historically have provided – but few are likely to offer unequivocal guarantees. The risk of service non-availability and its potential consequences,[12] as well as the options for mitigating any damage, must therefore be determined and evaluated.

Given that most Cloud providers are likely to be data processors, Recital 81 of the GDPR must be taken into account. This states that:

> To ensure compliance with the requirements of this Regulation in respect of the processing to be carried out by the processor on behalf of the controller, when entrusting a processor with processing activities, the controller should use only processors providing sufficient guarantees, in particular in terms of expert knowledge, reliability and resources, to implement technical and organisational measures which will meet the requirements of this Regulation, including for the security of processing.

Although physical inspection of a Cloud provider's "technical and organisational measures" is unlikely to be practical, all reasonable steps must be taken to verify that the provider's security measures are at least sufficient. This should be done by someone with an appropriate level of technical expertise, who is able to ask the right questions and understand the implications of the answers. Without that, it is much more likely that the data controller would be penalised should a breach occur.

If the Cloud provider already has some form of external certification, such as ISO 27001, this would make checking significantly easier. If the provider claims to have ISO 27001 certification, you could simply ask to see the certificate and the Statement of Applicability (SoA), which would allow you to verify the controls in place; in particular, you could check if the provider took note of Cloud-specific standards and guidance (discussed in more detail later in this chapter).

Areas to assess include:

- How access rights are authorised;

---

[12] Note that this is a risk the NIS Directive attempts to mitigate.

- How users are authenticated;
- Background checks and segregation of duties for the Cloud provider's personnel; and
- Physical access monitoring and segregation of data.

Although the security offered by providers is, of course, crucial, security of Cloud-based systems must start at the customer or data controller end. The controller should first get internal matters in order, after which it should carry out due diligence on the security provisions made by the Cloud provider.

In the Cloud, security must be managed differently. On an internal server it may be possible to rely heavily on perimeter defences. However, many security products cannot be deployed in a shared environment, and other organisations may use less secure applications within the perimeter of the Cloud service and endanger valuable data. Application-level and 'instance' security should therefore be considered. This could include:

- Firewalls or antivirus software that operate within each instance;
- Ensuring that system services are run only where necessary;
- Intrusion detection systems (IDS) and/or intrusion prevention systems (IPS); and
- Integrity checking or change monitoring software.

Where data is stored partly in the Cloud and partly in-house, proper classification of data is vitally important to determine what can safely be stored where, in accordance with legislation, standards, security concerns and the value of the asset.

Cyber Essentials

As discussed earlier, the most ideal situation would be for the Cloud provider to conform to an external scheme. One such example is the UK government's Cyber Essentials scheme, introduced in June 2014.[13] Although a good scheme, it may be of limited value in a Cloud provider's context, as it is only proof of a basic level of security, and – crucially – doesn't adequately address Cloud-specific risks.

Cyber Essentials sets out the basic controls that all organisations of any size should implement to counter the most common Internet-based security threats. It concentrates on five key areas:

1. Boundary firewalls and Internet gateways
2. Secure configuration
3. User access control
4. Malware protection
5. Patch management

Many organisations will, of course, have already identified some or all of these as necessary and taken steps to address them. None of them are new or surprising issues, so there is no real excuse for failing to implement appropriate measures. What the Cyber Essentials scheme does offer is a means of proving that the necessary steps have been taken, through external assessment.

The scheme is intended to be affordable, even for small organisations. There are two levels of assessment. The basic certificate involves completing a questionnaire, which is externally reviewed before the certificate is awarded. The more advanced Cyber Essentials Plus is based on more costly external and internal testing. In each case, the certificate – which must be renewed annually – entitles the organisation to display a logo.

Access controls

It is worth reiterating that Article 32 of the GDPR requires "technical and organisational" security measures. Although many basic controls are at the technical end, access control clearly has a large organisational component.

---

[13] Information on this is available at: *www.cyberessentials.ncsc.gov.uk*.

Access controls must apply both to the systems that allow users to access Cloud applications and to the Cloud applications themselves. Article 32 of the GDPR requires protection against *unauthorised* access. There are many ways of authorising access, but the allocation of logon credentials that then determine the information the user can view or manipulate has to be a key element. Access privileges should be carefully considered so that users see no more information than they need to, and do not have access to functions that are not relevant to them.

This is especially true in the Cloud, where each user's location may be less well controlled. It is often worth considering additional precautions – such as two-factor authentication (2FA) – that require strong authentication for password recovery or modification, and impose restrictions on the IP addresses from which the application may be accessed, and/or restrictions on the times of day at which any given user is permitted to log in.

Good segmentation of the data in the Cloud system so that users are restricted in what they can view or modify – and especially in what they can download, print or export – also helps to mitigate risks. Access to administrative functions must, of course, receive particular attention, and you should also consider monitoring activity live, in order to flag up any unusual behaviour before it is too late.

Controlling access via personal devices, through a BYOD policy, is particularly important if there is any possibility that confidential or sensitive personal data may be taken from the Cloud and stored on the device. This could be, for example, in the form of emails or information in attachments. Spreadsheets used as informal small databases are a particular hazard. Strict access controls to the device are also essential if the Cloud application requires a logon that can be 'remembered' by the device. A BYOD policy should prohibit access to such Cloud services by any personal devices that are not secured by the most appropriate access controls available. The data controller should also reserve the right to verify the presence of access controls at reasonable opportunities.

This is not just a hypothetical risk. A survey[14] in June 2014 found that 75% of consumers who use social media on mobile devices are automatically logged in to their accounts, and even 23% of mobile banking users are automatically logged in. These risks may be acceptable for individuals to choose to take with their own data, but the figures emphasise that employers cannot assume that individuals have taken an appropriate approach to the security of personal devices on which corporate data may be held or accessed.

It is likely that personal devices may occasionally, or regularly, be used by others with the permission of the owner. In this case, it is essential that these additional users are unable to access any data derived from or held by Cloud applications. Ideally, the device should provide for individual logons and allow only authorised users to access confidential data and associated applications. Again, reservation of the right to verify that these conditions are met may be a reasonable condition of permitting access from the device to corporate Cloud data.

Other guidance and recommendations

There are, of course, many sources of security guidance. One of the main ones is ISO/IEC 27001:2013, but the Open Web Application Security Project (OWASP) can also provide valuable guidance on common vulnerabilities.

The OWASP Top 10 is an analysis, updated every three years, of the current most important vulnerabilities in web-based systems and the measures that should be taken to prevent them. The 2017 Top 10 are[15]:

1. Injection
2. Broken authentication

---

[14] Commissioned by the software company Intercede.

[15] The 2017 OWASP Top 10 can be found at: *www.owasp.org/index.php/Top_10-2017_Top_10*

3. Sensitive data exposure
4. XML external entities (XXE)
5. Broken access control
6. Security misconfiguration
7. Cross-site scripting (XSS)
8. Insecure deserialization
9. Using components with known vulnerabilities
10. Insufficient logging and monitoring

It is worth taking a broad view, rather than relying on just one source to identify the security areas that should be given attention; for instance, a number of these points are relevant to the Cyber Essentials controls.

You should consider regular independent vulnerability assessments and penetration testing to ensure that applications are protected from, at the very least, well-documented threats.

ISO 27001 – information security

The key international standard on information security is the ISO 27000 series, of which ISO 27001 is the overall framework laying out the specifications for a best-practice information security management system (ISMS).[16] Organisations can be externally audited and certified against the Standard, providing solid evidence that their security measures are effective.

Annex A in ISO 27001 sets out a reference control set covering the key security areas for any organisation. Many are directly relevant to Cloud computing, including:

- Access control (A.9);
- Information transfer (A.13.2);
- System acquisition, development and maintenance (A.14);

---

[16] Available at: *www.itgovernance.co.uk/shop/Product/isoiec-27001-2013-iso-27001-standard-isms-requirements*.

- Information security in supplier relationships (A.15.1); and

- Privacy and protection of personally identifiable information (A.18.1.4).

On top of Annex A, ISO 27017 may be of use: this standard provides expanded guidance for the Annex A controls in ISO 27001 to make the guidance more applicable to Cloud service providers.[17]

Where ISO 27017 mainly focuses on practices and takes a more general approach, the Cloud Security Alliance Cloud Controls Matrix (CSA CCM) is much more specific to the technologies typically used by Cloud providers.[18] As a control set, the CSA CCM also integrates well with ISO 27001.

ISO 27001 accreditation is available both to the data controller and any Cloud suppliers it may use. Many suppliers claim to be ISO 27001-conformant, but it is important to check:

- Has the Cloud provider been externally certified, or just self-assessed as compliant?

- Are the credentials of the certifying body satisfactory?

- Does the ISO 27001 certificate apply to the issues that concern the data that is intended to be placed in the Cloud application, as set out in the supplier's ISO 27001 SoA?

Data 'in transit'

Data is almost inevitably more at risk when it is 'in transit' rather than 'at rest', which is why information transfer merits a specific control in ISO 27001. Many of the ICO's monetary penalties

---

[17] Available at: *www.itgovernance.co.uk/shop/product/iso-27017-2015-information-security-controls-for-cloud-services*.

[18] Available at: *https://cloudsecurityalliance.org/group/cloud-controls-matrix*.

have involved data going astray in transit (in a range of situations, not always in the context of Cloud computing).

When considering a Cloud provider's security claims, it is important to check whether these apply equally to data at rest (i.e. while stored on the provider's servers) and data in transit, both between the customer and the Cloud provider, and between the Cloud provider and any subcontractors that may provide part of the service.

European Secure Cloud (ESCloud) Label

The German Federal Office for Information Security (BSI) and French Agence nationale de la sécurité des systèmes d'information (ANSSI) collaborated to develop the ESCloud Label.

National frameworks are of limited use to Cloud providers, because Cloud services tend to be offered across borders. Equally, national cyber security authorities are limited in authority to their own country. The ESCloud Label is meant to provide a solution, as "the national safety certificates are combined under one roof and made comparable", taking into account key requirements of multiple Member States.[19] With time, the BSI and ANSSI hope to include members from more countries, making the framework more relevant from an international perspective. This would also be good news for Cloud users, as it provides assurance that the Cloud provider in question has security measures that meet more than just local standards.

Some other countries have localised schemes that Cloud providers can use; for instance, both the BSI and ANSSI have also developed or are developing their own standards. The BSI

---

[19] BSI, "European Secure Cloud Label (ESCloud Label)", *www.bsi.bund.de/EN/Topics/CloudComputing/ESCloudLabel/ESCloud Label_node.html*.

has its Cloud Computing Compliance Controls Catalogue (C5),[20] while the ANSSI is close to releasing its SecNumCloud.

Government agencies, or organisations that have close dealings with government, may want to review the Cloud provider's offering against relevant frameworks. For instance, the UK government uses its G-Cloud framework on its 'Digital Marketplace'.[21]

COBIT®

COBIT is another framework for information technology management and governance. It is seen as a way to fulfil the requirements of regulatory regimes (such as the US Sarbanes-Oxley Act) for risk mitigation, monitoring and control. COBIT 5 was released in June 2012. It is published by ISACA® (originally the Information Systems Audit and Control Association) and its components include:

- Framework, linking IT to business requirements;
- Organisation-wide process descriptions that map to responsibility for different aspects of the process;
- High-level control objectives;
- Management guidelines that include measuring performance; and
- Maturity models to assess systems and address gaps.

Additional BYOD considerations

The data controller will not usually be able to control which other applications are installed on personal devices. As such,

---

[20] Available at:
www.bsi.bund.de/EN/Topics/CloudComputing/Compliance_Controls_Catalogue/Compliance_Controls_Catalogue_node.html.

[21] At the time of writing, the latest version is G-Cloud 10 (updated in 2018), available at *www.gov.uk/guidance/g-cloud-templates-and-legal-documents*.

there is a risk of malicious or ill-behaved applications introducing security vulnerabilities. Strict data and application segregation can mitigate these risks.

If data can be downloaded from the Cloud to the device, it will be vulnerable to access by other users – with or without permission. Unwise behaviour by the device owner could result, for example, in the device being disposed of while still containing recoverable confidential information. It is also less likely that information updated on the device will be reliably backed up.

It is commonplace for devices – especially smartphones, which are particularly vulnerable to loss or theft – to allow remote locking and wiping of all data. A device owner may be reluctant to provide the data controller with the codes necessary to carry out these operations, or to inform the data controller as soon as the device's whereabouts are unknown. This is especially true if data is not segregated, meaning that the owner's personal information would be wiped at the same time.

For these reasons, it would be best to provide employees with company-issued phones wherever possible. An alternative is to require the device to use an application that ringfences data acquired from the organisation's systems, preventing it from being stored on the device, exported from it, or interfered with by other applications on the device. However, again, human factors must be taken into account. For example, a user who finds it onerous to enter a PIN or other security requirement each time they access the device, may be inclined to disengage the access controls after they have been authorised to use the device for accessing their employer's data.

CHAPTER 6: TRANSFERS TO THIRD COUNTRIES

If personal data is transferred to countries outside the EEA (called third countries in the GDPR) or international organisations, the provisions of Chapter V of the GDPR come into play. Storing data on a Cloud provider's system outside the EEA counts as such a transfer, even if the data is not intended to be used anywhere outside the EEA.

As discussed earlier, it is common for a Cloud application to be provided by a chain of subcontractors. It is the controller's responsibility to examine the entire chain in order to assess whether Chapter V applies. This chapter aims to achieve an equivalent level of protection for data transferred abroad to that it would receive within the EEA.

This level of protection is automatically provided if the jurisdiction to which the data is transferred is within the EEA, which comprises the EU plus Iceland, Liechtenstein and Norway.

Beyond that, a slowly increasing number of territories have legislation that has been assessed by the EC as providing an acceptable level of protection – in other words, the Commission has made an 'adequacy decision' as per Article 45.[22] As a special case, the US has negotiated the EU-US Privacy Shield (the successor to the Safe Harbor framework), as discussed in detail below.

This means that, at the time of writing, transfers to anywhere shown in *Table 1* are treated no differently, from a data protection perspective, than a transfer within the EEA.

---

[22] See *https://ec.europa.eu/info/law/law-topic/data-protection/data-transfers-outside-eu/adequacy-protection-personal-data-non-eu-countries_en* for the most up-to-date information.

Table 1: Third countries to which data can be transferred under the GDPR

Approved by EC	Andorra, Argentina, Canada (commercial organisations), Faroe Islands, Guernsey, Isle of Man, Israel, Japan,[23] Jersey, New Zealand, Switzerland, Uruguay
Special case	US, but only where the Privacy Shield applies

Transfers to almost all of Europe are therefore automatically compliant with Chapter V, one way or another, but the same does not apply to many others. A few countries, including Australia, Hong Kong, Morocco, Singapore and South Korea, have their own data protection laws, but these have not yet been approved by the EC.[24] It is important to reiterate that, as data controller, you need to make sure that you are aware of all countries in which the Cloud service provider operates; there is a strong possibility that the data in the Cloud moves between different locations – and you are responsible for ensuring that all these transfers are GDPR compliant.

Transfers outside the locations in the table above are only permitted if they meet one of the exemptions set out in Chapter V of the Regulation. These include:

---

[23] The adoption procedure of Japan's adequacy decision launched on 5 September 2018. The EC will adopt the adequacy decision on Japan once this procedure has been completed. *https://ec.europa.eu/info/law/law-topic/data-protection/data-transfers-outside-eu/adequacy-protection-personal-data-non-eu-countries_en*

[24] For an updated overview of data protection laws around the world, see *www.dlapiperdataprotection.com*.

- Having "appropriate safeguards" in place (Article 46), including binding corporate rules (Article 47) and standard contractual clauses;

- Explicit consent of the data subject, or protecting the vital interests of the data subject if they are unable to give consent;

- Necessity in connection with a contract (or prospective contract) between the data subject and the data controller, or a contract with another party at the request of the data subject;

- Necessity for reasons of substantial public interest; and

- Necessity for establishing, exercising or defending legal claims.

If you are relying on data subject consent, you must make your data subjects fully aware that you intend to transfer their data abroad, so that they can make their own decision on whether the risk is acceptable. In most Cloud computing situations, consent is unlikely to be a practicable option.

Necessity in relation to the performance of a contract is unlikely to be an acceptable claim in respect of Cloud computing, because it can always be argued that equivalent Cloud services could have been obtained from providers within the EEA.

Ensuring "adequate safeguards" are likely to be your best option and should be secured from the Cloud provider through contractual arrangements approved by the EC or supervisory authority. However, as ever, the data controller will be responsible for having to demonstrate that appropriate steps have been taken and that the terms and conditions, which the Cloud service more than likely will provide, actually do provide adequate safeguards.

A note on Brexit

At the time of writing, the UK is still part of the EU, and data can therefore be freely transferred to and from the UK under the GDPR. However, after Brexit, the UK will become a third country – despite having enshrined the Regulation's requirements in national law. That said, the latter may help it achieve an adequacy decision, or at least help ensure that organisations already have adequate safeguards in place.

EU-US Privacy Shield

Some commentators seriously questioned whether the Safe Harbor scheme in the US provided an adequate basis for data protection compliance when using Cloud services, and even though the scheme has since been thrown out and replaced with the EU-US Privacy Shield, this new scheme has also been challenged by, among others, the Article 29 Data Protection Working Party (WP29).[25]

Both schemes were designed to provide a basis for transferring data between the US and Europe that did not require the US government to put a data protection regime in place. However, despite the improvements, there are several drawbacks highlighted in the Privacy Shield's first annual review, including[26]:

- It is largely self-assessed and lacks clear guidance;
- The general lack of supervision; and
- The different interpretations of 'processing activities' by US processors and EU controllers.

Despite this, the agreement is at the time of writing still accepted by the EU as providing an adequate level of protection. If a Cloud provider based in the US is signed up to the Privacy Shield, therefore, the risk of being found in breach of Article 32 appears to be very small.

---

[25] Out-Law, "Data watchdogs threaten legal challenge to Privacy Shield unless oversight mechanisms are strengthened", December 2017, *www.out-law.com/en/articles/2017/december/data-watchdogs-threaten-legal-challenge-to-privacy-shield-unless-oversight-mechanisms-are-strengthened/*.

[26] WP29, "EU – U.S. Privacy Shield – First annual Joint Review", November 2017, *http://ec.europa.eu/newsroom/just/document.cfm?doc_id=48782*.

Some government data, however, is required to be held within the EEA, or even within specific Member States. There are also some data controllers that prefer not to rely on the Privacy Shield scheme. In these cases, a Cloud service where the data is guaranteed to be held only within the EEA would be preferable.

Until recently, this was easier said than done. Many of the big providers either refused to say where their data was held (for 'security' reasons), or explicitly stated that it would be held in the US. Now, though, many have accepted that there is a commercial advantage in providing at least the option for data to be held only within the EEA, and it is rare to find a service that holds all its data in the US, come what may. This is likely to only grow with the additional NIS Directive requirements imposed on Cloud providers offering their service in the EU, and gives even more reason for EU data controllers to look for local Cloud providers.

Data comes under the EU data protection regime as soon as it is held within Europe, even if it originates outside Europe, relates to data subjects outside Europe and is essentially only used outside Europe.

CHAPTER 7: DATA SUBJECTS' RIGHTS

Earlier in this book, it was mentioned that, with the introduction of the GDPR, data subjects have had their rights expanded, and that this may have a significant impact on Cloud users.

All eight data subject rights are listed in Articles 13–22:

1. *The right to be informed*

The data subject must be given specific information about how and why their personal data will be processed. Depending on how you use Cloud services, this may include, for instance, mentioning that the personal data will be transferred to a third country.

2. *The right of access*

Data subjects can ask for all the personal data you hold on them – including the data held in the Cloud. Note that there are very few exceptions; the most common ones are usually associated with protecting the confidentiality of other individuals.

3. *The right to rectification*

The data subject may ask for their data to be corrected and/or completed. If they exercise this right, you have to ensure that this information is corrected everywhere – again, this includes duplicates that might be stored in the Cloud or in other remote locations.

4. *The right to erasure (the 'right to be forgotten')*

In certain cases, the data subject can ask you to delete all data you hold on them. This right is extensive but not without limitations.

5. *The right to restriction of processing*

In some circumstances, the data subject may require that processing of their data be restricted or suppressed. This means you may store but not use the data. These cases are limited, but if they apply, you have no choice but to comply.

6.   *The right to data portability*

Under specific conditions, subjects may ask for their data to be provided in "a structured, commonly used and machine-readable format", which they may also ask to be transferred to another data controller.

7.   *The right to object*

In certain scenarios, particularly for direct marketing, data subjects may object to their data being processed. Unless the controller can show that it has legitimate grounds, it must stop processing that data.

8.   *Rights in relation to automated decision-making and profiling*

The GDPR places strict controls on the use of automated decision-making based on personal data. This is supported by a set of rights that the data subject can invoke to prevent that processing.

If a data subject exercises their right to submit a 'subject access request' (SAR), controllers are obliged to respond within one calendar month, and to provide *all* data they hold on that data subject.

Naturally, accommodating an SAR is a more complex process if you hold or process the subject's data in the Cloud, as Cloud applications and services may store caches in locations you are unaware of or cannot easily access. Furthermore, wide usage of Cloud technologies throughout the organisation can result in copies of data – that are not completely identical to the local version – that are not easily tracked or identified.

You must also be able to track down personal data if a data subject exercises their right to rectification or right to be forgotten. In either case, their data will not just have to be corrected or deleted locally, but also in the Cloud – which, as mentioned above, could involve locating duplicated personal data.

To help locate all your data, you should consider performing a data mapping exercise. If you have identified all data flows, it will be significantly easier and quicker to facilitate a data subject exercising their rights.

On top of this, you should put an SAR process in place to locate *all* data, which may be held in emails, in a timely manner. This ensures that you do not miss data that may, for instance, be backed up as part of the Cloud service. More to the point, having an effective, documented process ensures you maintain good oversight and can demonstrate your compliance.

If you fail to accommodate the SAR or fail to do so within the one-month timeframe and do not give reasons for the delay, your organisation could be subject to the higher-level GDPR fines: up to €20 million or 4% of global annual turnover – whichever is greater.

CHAPTER 8: OTHER LEGAL AND TECHNICAL IMPLICATIONS FOR CLOUD CONTRACTS

We have already discussed the requirements for a contract between a data controller and a data processor, as well as the contractual implications when Cloud processors are based outside the EEA. This chapter looks briefly at other legal and technical issues with data protection implications.

Naturally, while security is important, ensuring that the data is available when required is also a crucial point. Problems could arise from:

- Loss of service:
  - At the provider's end, if their system goes down; or
  - At the customer's end, if the Internet connection is impaired.
- Possible obstacles to a change of provider if the service proves unsatisfactory, caused by the data being held in a proprietary format;
- Possible difficulty retrieving the data if the service ceases, or in case of a dispute with the provider; or
- Difficulty in making a usable and comprehensive backup of the data independently from the provider's system, as additional security in case of problems.

Even though the NIS Directive stipulates that Cloud service providers must put "appropriate and proportionate technical and organisational measures" in place to "manage the risks posed" (Article 16(1)), which must take incident handling and business continuity into account, Cloud providers are unlikely to offer *guaranteed* levels of service, as failures do happen from time to time. Because these risks cannot be ignored, you should ensure contingency plans are in place. This is why the Directive is ultimately about cyber resilience – not just protecting what can be protected, but also ensuring that the organisation is able to recover from any incidents.

Also note that under the NIS Directive, incidents of "substantial impact" have to be reported. However, it is the Cloud service provider's responsibility to assess the scale of the incident (thereby determining whether it should be reported) – not the supervisory body, and not the data controller.

Retrieving data in the event of a breakdown in the commercial relationship may be less easy to provide for, which is why a readily usable backup, independent of the Cloud provider's systems, is likely to be essential. Not only may the format in which data is stored make retrieval of useful data awkward, there is also the question of precisely where it is stored and how to access it.

Few Cloud providers control all the assets involved in providing their service. Frequently, there are several links in the chain: the service provider may be a reseller of another company's product; the data storage may be subcontracted out, and the subcontractor may not own the physical hardware on which the data is stored. Should any of these links break, there is no direct contract between the data controller and the ultimate holder of the data. To complicate matters further, the different companies in the chain may be based in different legal jurisdictions.

Other points to watch out for in standard terms and conditions include:

- Contract terms that make the supplier a data controller in their own right (for example, if they reserve the right to make use of the customer's data, or some of it, for their own purposes); and

- Unilateral changes in terms and conditions by the provider.

These concerns all indicate that it is very important to carefully study the legal and technical underpinning of any Cloud service before entrusting personal data to it – for which you may be held liable – or basing critical processes on Cloud applications. It is not always easy to piece together all the necessary information, and some providers are better than others at making such details all readily available in a comprehensible form. A cursory review is not enough, and those entrusted with the review should have the necessary legal or technical expertise to understand the implications of the information they obtain.

The concerns also contribute to an essential requirement in any Cloud application: ensuring that there is a reliable way to continue business if the relationship with the Cloud provider breaks down in any way. An escrow or recovery procedure should not just be put in place, but also tested and documented so that it can be reliably and promptly brought into action if required.

Ideally, such a procedure should be built into an incident management programme that takes note of both ISO 27001 and ISO 27035 – the Standard for information security incident response.[27] If communication with a Cloud provider does break down, this is likely to have a serious impact; as such, it may be a good idea to prepare for this as a specific scenario within such a management programme.

Responding to breaches

The UK's ICO provides information on security breaches[28] and checklists for organisations to prepare for and effectively respond to data breaches in line with the GDPR.[29]

Most organisations will be concerned at the reputational damage that a serious breach would be likely to bring. It is common practice to have a prepared statement in place that can be adapted to the specific circumstances, and to allocate responsibility for

---

[27] You may wish to consult IT Governance's Cyber Incident Response Management service, available at: *www.itgovernance.co.uk/shop/Product/cyber-incident-response-management*.

[28] ICO, "Security breaches", *https://ico.org.uk/for-organisations/guide-to-pecr/communications-networks-and-services/security-breaches/*.

[29] ICO, "Personal data breaches", *https://ico.org.uk/for-organisations/guide-to-the-general-data-protection-regulation-gdpr/personal-data-breaches/*.

communications with the media and with regulators. It may be worth considering whether arrangements should also be made to involve the Cloud provider in the response, if the breach takes place as a result of a failure for which they are partly or wholly responsible.

With regard to Cloud services, there are other considerations in the wake of a breach. For instance, are you able to segregate systems provided in the Cloud? Do you have reliable access to backups? Does the provider have adequate resources to support recovery and to provide logs and other evidence? If the breach results in a 'simple' loss of functionality, does the Cloud provider offer guarantees of continuity? All these questions should be considered when preparing your organisation for a breach.

CHAPTER 9: CHECKLIST

Throughout this book, various recommendations have been made. They are summarised here for convenience.

☐ Before embarking on a Cloud computing development, ensure that your organisation's information (and especially IT) security framework is sound, and that responsibility for information security is clearly allocated.

☐ Ensure that your organisation's approach to data protection compliance is well thought out, and that responsibility is clearly allocated.

☐ Before selecting a Cloud provider, consider whether your data needs to be retained in the EEA, and if so, make this a key selection criterion.

☐ For all Cloud providers under consideration, check the contract (or standard terms and conditions) very carefully, especially for:

- Ownership of the data;
- Security undertakings and certified security standards;
- Location of data and whether you have any control over this;
- Any mention of liability the provider accepts or excludes;
- Any mention of whether the provider uses subcontractors;
- Arrangements for you to make your own backups, in addition to those made automatically by the provider;
- How you obtain access to your data in the event of wanting to change provider;
- What happens to your data if the provider (or one of its subcontractors) goes out of business, or if you get into a dispute with the provider;

- Any provision for the supplier to use your data for its own purposes; and
- Mechanisms by which you can verify, for example, where the data is held.

☐ Verify any claims made by the providers for compliance with, for example:

- The GDPR and/or NIS Directive;
- ISO 27001; or
- The EU-US Privacy Shield, in the case of a US-based organisation.

☐ It is impossible to eliminate all risks. Assess the risks and prepare a risk assessment so that the appropriate people in your organisation can make an informed decision.

☐ Ensure that any contractors assisting in setting up the Cloud application are given clear instructions about the security measures they should be implementing.

☐ Once the Cloud service is in place, consider commissioning external testing to ensure that it has been configured correctly and is not vulnerable to any well-documented security threats.

☐ Ensure that access to the Cloud application and the data it holds is adequately controlled, especially if it may be accessed by users working at home or on their own devices.

☐ Provide adequate training and guidance for all users so that they know both how to use the system and how to ensure that personal data placed in it is appropriately handled.

REFERENCES

Sumner Blount and Rob Zanella, *Cloud Security and Governance: Who's on your Cloud?*, *IT Governance Publishing*, 2010.

Lee Newcombe, *Securing Cloud Services: A pragmatic approach to security architecture in the Cloud*, IT Governance Publishing, 2012.

Jared Carstensen, JP Morgenthal and Bernard Golden, *Cloud Computing: Assessing the risks*, IT Governance Publishing, 2012.

Kevin T. McDonald, *Above the Clouds: Managing Risk in the World of Cloud Computing*, IT Governance Publishing, 2010.

Renzo Marchini, *Cloud Computing: A Practical Introduction to the Legal Issues*, BSI Standards, 2010.

www.cloudsecurityalliance.org (CCM Framework).

FURTHER READING

IT Governance Publishing (ITGP) is the world's leading publisher for governance and compliance. Our industry-leading pocket guides, books, training resources and toolkits are written by real-world practitioners and thought leaders. They are used globally by audiences of all levels, from students to C-suite executives.

Our high-quality publications cover all IT governance, risk and compliance frameworks and are available in a range of formats. This ensures our customers can access the information they need in the way they need it.

Our other publications related to the subjects covered in this pocket guide include:

- EU GDPR: A pocket guide, second edition
  www.itgovernancepublishing.co.uk/product/eu-gdpr-a-pocket-guide-second-edition
- Network and Information Security (NIS) Regulations - A pocket guide for digital service providers
  www.itgovernancepublishing.co.uk/product/network-and-information-systems-nis-regulations-a-pocket-guide-for-digital-service-providers
- Securing Cloud Services – A pragmatic approach to security architecture in the Cloud
  www.itgovernancepublishing.co.uk/product/securing-cloud-services

For more information on ITGP and to view our full list of publications, please visit

www.itgovernancepublishing.co.uk.

To receive regular updates from ITGP, including information on new publications in your area(s) of interest, sign up for our newsletter at
www.itgovernancepublishing.co.uk/topic/newsletter.

Branded publishing

Through our branded publishing service, you can customise ITGP publications with your company's branding.

Find out more at
www.itgovernancepublishing.co.uk/topic/branded-publishing-services.

Related services

ITGP is part of GRC International Group, which offers a comprehensive range of complementary products and services to help organisations meet their objectives.

For a full range of resources on the subjects covered in this pocket guide, please visit the following pages:
www.itgovernance.co.uk/cloud-computing
www.itgovernance.co.uk/data-protection-dpa-and-eu-data-protection-regulation
www.itgovernance.co.uk/nis-directive.

Training services

The IT Governance training programme is built on our extensive practical experience designing and implementing management systems based on ISO standards, best practice and regulations.

Our courses help attendees develop practical skills and comply with contractual and regulatory requirements. They also support career development via recognised qualifications.

Learn more about our training courses and view the full course catalogue at
www.itgovernance.co.uk/training.

Professional services and consultancy

We are a leading global consultancy of IT governance, risk management and compliance solutions. We advise businesses around the world on their most critical issues and present cost-saving and risk-reducing solutions based on international best practice and frameworks.

We offer a wide range of delivery methods to suit all budgets, timescales and preferred project approaches.

Find out how our consultancy services can help your organisation at *www.itgovernance.co.uk/consulting*.

Industry news

Want to stay up to date with the latest developments and resources in the IT governance and compliance market? Subscribe to our Daily Sentinel newsletter and we will send you mobile-friendly emails with fresh news and features about your preferred areas of interest, as well as unmissable offers and free resources to help you successfully start your projects: *www.itgovernance.co.uk/daily-sentinel.*

EU for product safety is Stephen Evans, The Mill Enterprise Hub, Stagreenan, Drogheda, Co. Louth, A92 CD3D, Ireland. (servicecentre@itgovernance.eu)